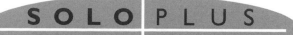

SOLO PLUS

Trumpet

with piano accompaniment

T0066064

My First Recital

Trumpet

with piano accompaniment

An outstanding collection of twenty-three light classics and folk songs
from around the world expertly arranged for the first-time recitalist.
With piano accompaniment in printed *and* digitally recorded formats.

Cover photography by Randall Wallace
Arranged and performed by David Pearl

Order No. AM 947463
US International Standard Book Number: 0.8256.1683.2
UK International Standard Book Number: 0.7119.6954.X

Exclusive Distributors:
Music Sales Corporation
257 Park Avenue South, New York, NY 10010 USA
Music Sales Limited
8/9 Frith Street, London W1V 5TZ England
Music Sales Pty. Limited
120 Rothschild Street, Rosebery, Sydney, NSW 2018, Australia

Printed in the United States of America by
Vicks Lithograph and Printing Corporation

Amsco Publications
New York/London/Sydney

Contents

A Frangesa

Costa

Tempo di marcia ♩= 96

A Media Luz

E. Donato

Tango ♩ = 100

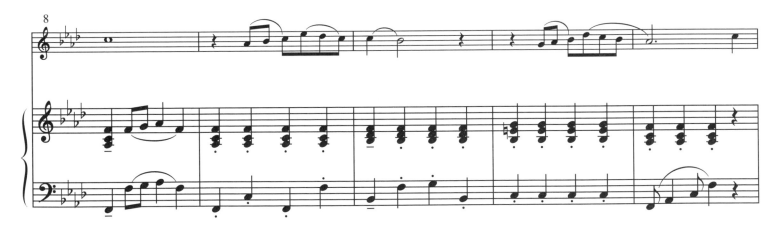

Allemande

Franz Joseph Haydn

Moderato ♩ = 120

Amaryllis

H. Ghys

Allegro moderato ♩ = 96

Arirang

Korean Folk Song

The Beautiful Jasmine

Ancient Chinese Melody

Bourée

Leopold Mozart

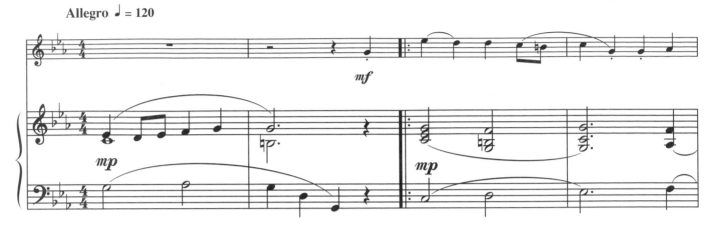

El Coqui

Puerto Rican Folk Song

Dubula

Shoot

African Folk Song

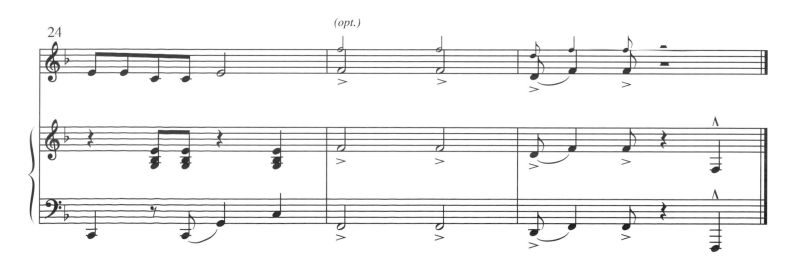

Grand March
from *Aida*

Giuseppe Verdi

Allegro maestoso ♩= 96

The Cowherd's Song

Edvard Grieg

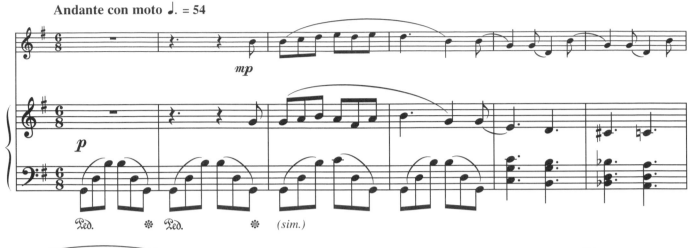

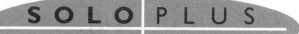

Trumpet

Cover photography by Randall Wallace
Arranged and performed by David Pearl

Order No. AM 947463
US International Standard Book Number: 0.8256.1683.2
UK International Standard Book Number: 0.7119.6954.X

Exclusive Distributors:
Music Sales Corporation
257 Park Avenue South, New York, NY 10010 USA
Music Sales Limited
8/9 Frith Street, London W1V 5TZ England
Music Sales Pty. Limited
120 Rothschild Street, Rosebery, Sydney, NSW 2018, Australia

Printed in the United States of America by
Vicks Lithograph and Printing Corporation

Amsco Publications
New York/London/Sydney

Contents

A Frangesa

Costa

A Media Luz

E. Donato

4

Allemande

Franz Joseph Haydn

Moderato ♩ = 120

Amaryllis

H. Ghys

Allegro moderato ♩ = 96

5

Arirang

Korean Folk Song

5

The Beautiful Jasmine

Ancient Chinese Melody

Bourée

Leopold Mozart

Allegro ♩ = 120

El Coqui

Puerto Rican Folk Song

Moderately ♩. = 48

Dubula
Shoot

African Folk Song

Grand March
from *Aida*

Giuseppe Verdi

Allegro maestoso ♩= 96

The Cowherd's Song

Edvard Grieg

Andante con moto ♩. = 54

The Happy Farmer

Robert Schumann

Moderato ♩ = 88

Matilda

Jamaican Folk Song

Merry Widow Waltz

Franz Lehár

Harmony Rag

Hal Nichols

Plaisir d'Amour

Giovanni Martini

Minuet
from *Violin Concerto K. 219*

Wolfgang Amadeus Mozart

Rondo Aragonesa

Allegro ♩ = 138

Enrique Granados

Slovakian Dance Tune

Traditional

Lively ♩ = 104

Song of Kokkiriko

Japanese Folk Song

Moderately slow ♩= 84

Solace

Scott Joplin

Very slow march

Song of the North

Edvard Grieg

Moderato ♩. = 56

Trio

Johann Sebastian Bach

Andantino espressivo ♩ = 84

The Happy Farmer

Robert Schumann

Moderato ♩= 88

Matilda

Jamaican Folk Song

Moderately slow calypso ♩= 69

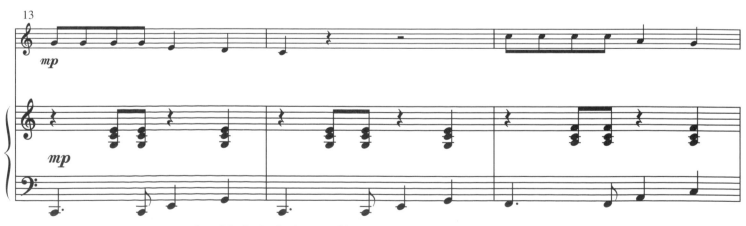

Merry Widow Waltz

Franz Lehár

Tempo di valse, molto tranquillo ♩. = 60

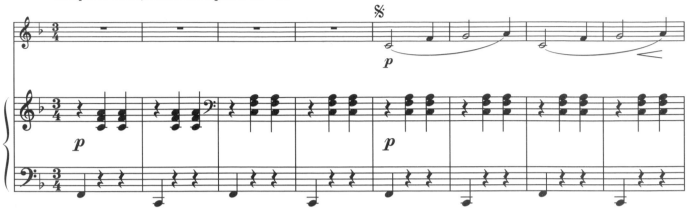

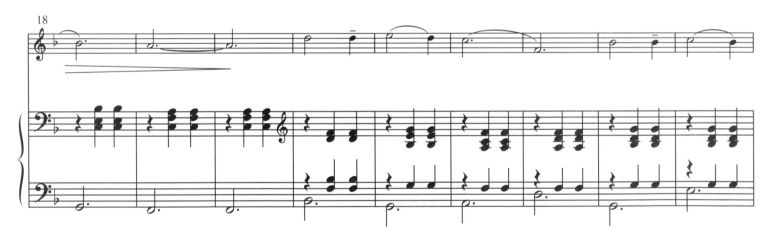

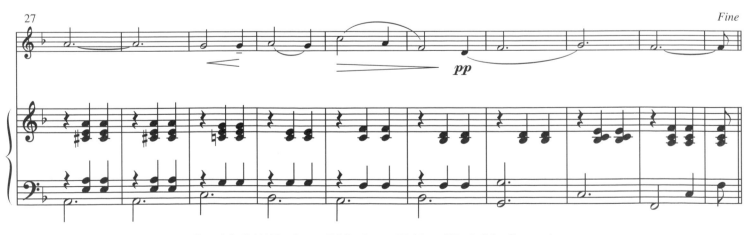

D.S. al Fine

Harmony Rag

Hal Nichols

Plaisir d'Amour

Giovanni Martini

Allegretto grazioso ♪ = 98

Minuet
from *Violin Concerto K. 219*

Wolfgang Amadeus Mozart

Tempo di minuetto ♩ = 88

Rondo Aragonesa

Enrique Granados

Allegro ♩ = 138

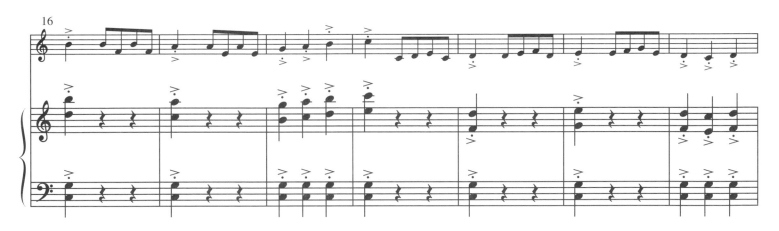

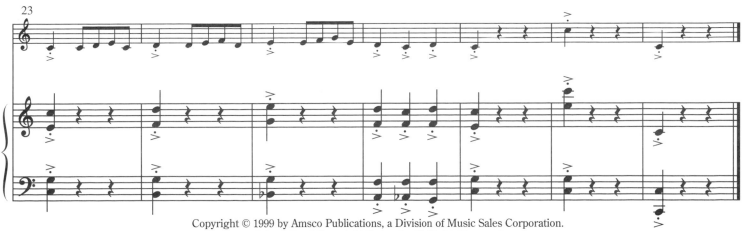

Slovakian Dance Tune

Traditional

Song of Kokkiriko

Japanese Folk Song

Moderately slow ♩= 84

Solace

Scott Joplin

Very slow march

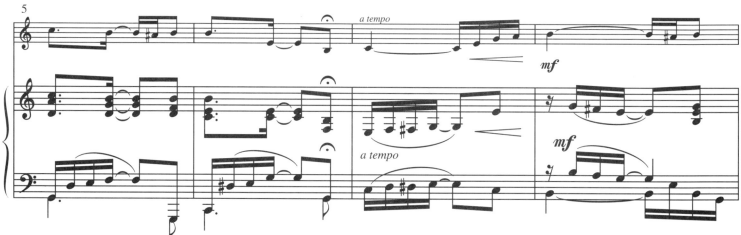

Song of the North

Edvard Grieg

Trio

Johann Sebastian Bach